Essentia
Evangelical
Spirituality

by
John Cockerton

formerly Principal of St. John's College, Durham

GROVE BOOKS LIMITED
Bramcote Nottingham NG9 3DS

Contents

FOREWORD

John Cockerton was ordained in 1954. After serving a curacy in St. Helens, he moved to Cranmer Hall to serve successively as tutor and warden, and then as Principal of St. John's College, Durham, of which Cranmer Hall is a constituent part. More recently he was in parish work.

In 1980 three members of the Grove Worship Group were moved by the need to affirm the specific contribution of evangelical spirituality within the Church. At the time, Anglicans of all sorts were exploring a variety of ways of getting to know God better. People asked us, 'Is there an evangelical spirituality?' Too readily they assumed it amounted to little more than the traditional individual walk with God, supported by a daily Quiet Time.

We invited John Cockerton to speak to our first gathering at St. John's College, Nottingham. He spoke to us clearly of the distinctive contributions of what he called 'mystical' spirituality on the one hand, and 'evangelical' spirituality on the other.

Fourteen years and 49 booklets later we have persuaded John to develop some of the points he made at our first meeting. He has immersed himself in the evangelical tradition of spiritual life and devotion. He speaks with wisdom and authority. It has been one of the main purposes of the Grove Spirituality Group, throughout its existence, to draw on the same well of spiritual life which is a continual source of renewal in the Church.

Ian Bunting

The Cover Picture is by Patrick Duncan
First Impression May 1994
ISSN 0262-799X
ISBN 1 85174 267 0

1
Introduction

Our title is not without its difficulties. In the first place, what is meant by
'spirituality' here? One definition might be, and indeed has been: 'the theology and practice of prayer'. Another definition, wider and arguably more
satisfactory, is: 'the whole life of the Christian as lived in the presence of God
and for God'. T.R. Albin in the *New Dictionary of Theology* gives a similar definition of Christian spirituality. It involves, he says, 'the relationship between
the whole person and a holy God, who reveals himself through both Testa-
ments — and supremely in the person of his unique Son, Jesus Christ'. One
might regard the first definition (prayer) as too narrow and the second
(Christian life) as too broad to be meaningful. In fact the large body of modern literature on spirituality reveals how many and varied are the under-
standings of the subject. The present study tries to recognize the breadth of it
while at the same time, because of the limitations both of space and of the
competence of the author, it concentrates on just a few themes. We will pro-
ceed with a definition which leaves loose ends in all directions but which is
sufficiently serviceable for our present purpose. We shall treat 'spirituality'
as that way of regarding Christian living which highlights and articulates
the believer's personal relationship to God. Since all Christian spirituality,
from whatever tradition it comes, is based on the understanding of such a
personal relationship (whether the precise definition is broad or narrow) this
will do as an indication of what we are about.

And what of the adjective, 'Evangelical'? There has always been variety
in Evangelicalism from the Reformation onwards. Just how one defines the
historical phenomenon is therefore problematical. Two things would seem to
be clear. First, the whole movement consciously adopts the fundamentals of
the faith as set out in the ecumenical creeds. Secondly, it has tended to concentrate on what is called the 'theology of the Christian life' (only in comparatively recent times has it engaged seriously with 'cultural' issues, as
adumbrated by the Dutch school which arose about 100 years ago). We
might well ask at what point in history such a survey should begin. There is
no agreement on the question. Since in this study we are not attempting an
historical account of Evangelical spirituality but merely attempting to characterize it by drawing out some of its leading features as these appear in
Anglicanism, we are under no obligation to tackle historical questions such
as this, even if it were possible! But we shall work with a tacit understanding
that Evangelical spirituality as we know it took its rise in the sixteenth century, with the work of the Reformers, though we shall be resting mostly on
the work of their spiritual successors in the following centuries. What then is

'Evangelicalism'? We can say that it is a complex of beliefs and practices. Much of what Evangelicals believe and do is also believed and done by people of other Christian traditions though there are some distinctives, like the doctrine of assurance. It is the total structure that is important, the bringing together of various building-blocks and the making out of them a building with its own particular shape and style. The distinctives are certainly present but these are quite often matters of emphasis rather than of straight difference.

Evangelical spirituality must be understood as cutting across the denominational divides but in this study we shall be looking almost exclusively at its Anglican (or, more correctly, its Church of England) manifestations. All spirituality gets its character from the putting together of devotion, discipline, liturgy and life (*New Dictionary of Theology*, article 'Spirituality'). Evangelical spirituality has its own particular way of doing this, its own distinctive style.

2

On Being Accepted

Bible-based Spirituality

We confront here a feature of Christian life which is not peculiar to Evangelicals. However, the central place of the Bible in the devotional life of Evangelicals is such a strong and historically consistent characteristic of their tradition that it is appropriate to give it special mention. That it should be so prominent a feature of Evangelical devotional life is not at all surprising, in view of the emphasis which the tradition lays on the authority of Scripture for the whole life of the Church and of the individual Christian. In their introduction to a recently published volume on *Evangelical Anglicans*, the editors, R.T. France and A.E. McGrath, list four assumptions upon which Evangelicalism is centred. The first of these is: 'The authority and sufficiency of Scripture'. Evangelical insistence on the Bible as the Word of God (communicated indeed through human authors but not in such a way as to iron out their human characteristics — that is, not by a process of heavenly dictation) has made this 'assumption' decisively influential for every department of Evangelical thinking. So it is not surprising to find that in the case of spirituality the Bible has a vital part to play. The book just mentioned has some interesting chapters on the practice of biblical criticism by Evangelical scholars. The point has to be underlined, I think, that there is still, as there has always been, a large disparity between what the scholars are contributing and what the 'person in the pew' is receiving from them. Despite the much greater availability these days of straightforward studies of Bible books and Bible themes by people of unimpeachable scholarly credentials, my observation would be that Christian people are not benefiting as much as they might from the good things which are on offer. What can be done? I ask the question in the hope that others will answer!

In practice, many use the Bible with minimal reference to its historical background. But the accompanying use of carefully produced Bible reading aids like those published by the Bible Reading Fellowship and the Scripture Union and others have undoubtedly done a lot to inform daily readers, to correct misconceptions, and to unveil meanings that otherwise would have been obscure or completely hidden. Further, many Evangelicals (and they are not alone in this) have been enthusiastic about Bible study groups and have invested much time and energy in making them work to the spiritual benefit of all concerned. Evangelicalism has laid stress on the importance of the Bible for the spiritual growth of individuals and of congregations. As to the latter, it is certainly the case that the taste for biblical preaching in Evangelical congregations has been sharpened by the use of the Bible in private, and, conversely, the exposition of the Bible from the pulpit has encouraged people to read the Bible at home. The conviction that God actually speaks to people, revealing his historical purpose in Christ for the whole world, for the Church and for Christian individuals, needs to be undergirded by ever-increasing attention to the serious study of Holy Scripture. And the point needs to be made firmly (as the authors of the book mentioned themselves make it) that there is a *history* of biblical interpretation, there is a *tradition* of understanding the Bible to which all Christians, scholars and others, should give *reverent* attention. God truly speaks to individuals as they open their hearts and minds to him and listen to his Word, but they must never forget that they are set within the Church to which God has been pleased to give light and understanding over the centuries. Evangelicals have often been accused of 'individualism' at this point. They ought to be careful to see that their contemporary practice leaves no room for such a charge.

The Cross and Christian Realism

If, as is sometimes alleged, Evangelicals are not emphasizing as they once did the Cross of Christ, the charge is a serious one. Certainly the message of Christ crucified has historically been one of the outstanding marks of the Evangelical tradition. Preachers and theologians have majored on it, presenting it as both the divine remedy for sin and the needed paradigm of the continuing work of God in the world when viewed in the light of the resurrection. Whether in fact it is the case that Evangelicals across the denom-

5

inations are failing to give the centrality to this message that their forebears gave it I find it impossible to say. Others, who have a wider knowledge of the Church, are in a better position to judge. I simply repeat that *if* it is true it is a serious indictment of contemporary Evangelicalism, not only because it signals a departure from tradition but because it fails to do justice to the New Testament. Shortage of easy-to-read, up-to-date literature cannot be the problem. There are books like John Stott *The Cross of Christ* (deservedly hailed as a 'classic') and George Carey *The Gate of Glory*, and a number of others. Perhaps Evangelicals need to re-focus their minds on the Cross by reading books such as these, and perhaps those competent to do so will give us more literature particularly on the pressing issues concerning the relationship of Christ's Cross to the world's pain, at a time when people in general are being made much more aware than ever before, through the media, of the scale and horror of suffering.

The accent on joy these days in the worship of the Church and in the lives of individuals is surely to be welcomed. The church has all too often given the impression of being tired and bored with itself, and with its message. Much good has come, and is coming, thank God, from the note of celebration that now features so largely in the worship of not a few congregations; Christians have much to celebrate! But what precisely are they celebrating? Certainly the presence and power of the Holy Spirit, certainly the experience of the love of God shed abroad in Christian hearts, certainly the gifts and graces bestowed on the Church by the munificent Spirit. All these wonderful things. But do they not all have their source in the divine act of redemption which Christ wrought by his death and resurrection? Celebration goes askew if it does not put first things first. Christians rejoice in the dying and rising of Jesus because from that saving event come all the blessings they enjoy. '...we rejoice in God through our Lord Jesus Christ', says St. Paul in Romans 5.11, 'through whom we have now received reconciliation', and Charles Wesley turns that rejoicing into song in his great hymn, 'O for a thousand tongues to sing/my great Redeemer's praise,/the glories of my God and King,/the triumphs of his grace'. The great reconciliation effected at the Cross is the fount of Christian exultation. Evangelicals down the centuries have known that and given expression to it. How far is it recognized in Evangelicalism today?

I have alluded to 'the problem of pain'. One particular manifestation of this calls for mention. Any brand of spirituality must have something to say to the many hurting people who are sitting in the pews (*and* occupying the pulpit and the manse) if it is to be big enough and deep enough to deal with the enormous range of personal needs within the Church (let alone outside it). There would seem to be a crying need for a spirituality which helps people through the dark times in life when God seems to be absent and prayer

6

seems to be meaningless. Here there are resources in the Evangelical tradition which can bring a lot of help (see for reference to these, J.I. Packer *Among God's Giants*; Gaius Davies *Genius and Grace*; Alister McGrath *The Enigma of the Cross*). Christian realism demands that preachers and pastors and all who try to give help to their suffering fellow Christians should work from a spirituality which sees the Cross as the place *par excellence* where God shows his involvement in the world's sorrows. And sensitivity to the experience of God-forsakenness which Christians not infrequently endure demands that help be given from the perspective of the Cross, that place where God appeared to be totally absent but was actually (as the resurrection indicated) never more truly present. Let Evangelicals and those of other traditions too reckon with the severe difficulties which many Christians encounter in this area and try to alleviate them with the message of the Cross.

Acceptance with God

The doctrine of 'justification by faith' (more accurately, 'justification by grace through faith') is foundational for Evangelical spirituality. What it means, stated very simply, is that God through Christ has done all that needs to be done to enable men and women to come to him and to be fully and freely accepted by him, so that their relationship with him rests, not upon what *they* might achieve but on what *he* has already achieved, an achievement which they have simply to receive in faith. When this biblical truth is grasped and allowed to influence one's thinking and one's whole life before God there comes a sense of release and freedom which colours all of one's prayers and all of one's life as a Christian in the world. So Christians have found from the beginnings of the Church. The danger of allowing this understanding of a person's relationship with God to be obscured and supplanted by a very different one, that which makes the Christian work for divine acceptance, has always been present. From time to time individuals have warned about the danger and, at the Reformation in the sixteenth century, the alarm was widely and insistently raised and the doctrine of justification by faith given great prominence. Martin Luther called justification by faith the 'article of a standing or falling Church' [that is, the article by which the Church stands or falls], which indicates how foundational he judged it to be. Manifestly it was an 'article' that needed to be defined and presented with care because it was so easily misunderstood. Faith, for instance, does not hang in the air as if it were merely an exercise of the mind and heart with no objective referent. The faith in question is precisely faith in God through Christ. Hence, one of the English Reformation's most sturdy preachers, Hugh Latimer, urges his hearers

'Catch thou hold of our Saviour, believe in Him, be assured in thy heart that He with his suffering took away all thy sins...When we believe in Him it is like as if we had no sins.'

Further, to accept this doctrine is not to be granted *carte blanche* for behaviour which contradicts the relationship with God which the doctrine implies, as if we were to say, 'Now that I'm accepted by God's grace it doesn't matter how much I sin; indeed I can sin with impunity knowing that God will not reject me'. Incredible though it may seem, something very like this appears to have invaded Christian minds from time to time and still does. Exponents of the true doctrine have therefore been at pains to make clear that acceptance by God through Christ is the most powerful incentive to good living that one could possibly have, for how could one embrace one's acceptance and not wish to please God out of sheer gratitude for his welcome and his continuing generosity? The Christian's calling is to realize in practice, in daily living, by God's grace, all that is implied in being a member of God's family, one of the company of those whom he calls his own. In fact, as the lives of the saints show quite clearly, this calling has been heeded by those who have seen that justification by faith has large ethical and spiritual implications and have sought to live before God in humility and thankfulness. We may recall the parable of the 'Pharisee and the Tax Collector' in Luke 18, which Jesus told 'to some who were confident of their own righteousness and looked down on everybody else'. It was not the pharisee at prayer in the Temple, thanking God that he was not like other men and reminding God of his ascetic practice, but the tax collector with his prayer, 'God, have mercy on me, a sinner', uttered in an attitude of deep humility, who 'went home justified before God' (NIV).

There can be no doubt that the cultivation of this attitude, based on a proper appreciation of divine acceptance for Christ's sake, makes for spirituality that is joyful and free. The Evangelical tradition has always tried to promote this kind of spirituality with (of course) varying degrees of success. Not indeed that other traditions have neglected it even though they have sometimes allowed it to become overlaid. How heart-warming it is to read of this spirituality being commended today in the Roman Catholic church where, let it be said for the benefit of Protestants who may not be aware of the point, the greatest of the Catholic spiritual teachers have always tried carefully to preserve the primacy of grace. Father Raniero Cantalamessa, official preacher to the papal household for many years, conducted a retreat for bishops and clergy in 1993 at Leeds. He spoke on the theme of the lordship of Jesus Christ in the life of the Christian and, as reported in *The Tablet* of 24 April 1993, urged the priests to rediscover the revelation of what being justified by faith really meant for them personally, and restore this message to their preaching. He said that people had often been left with the impression that they had to earn their way to heaven by good works, rather than that salvation was a free gift, with works a sign of the Holy Spirit in a person's life, not a way to earn grace. As one reads this one is prompted to say, 'Let all Christians, Evangelicals included (who may have been losing their sense of the importance of this teaching), pay heed and make an active response'. Clearly this is not a doctrine peculiar to Evangelicals though historically it has been a characteristic mark of their theology and their preaching. It is certainly the way to peace and spiritual freedom and, as the Reformers and their Evangelical successors insistently urge, it is vital for the spiritual health of the whole Church. In these ecumenical days it would be good if this teaching were to take fresh hold on Christian hearts and minds across the denominations.

Being Sure

Evangelical insistence on the importance of being sure in the faith has often been put down by its critics as presumptuousness. True, it has sometimes appeared as a rather unpleasant cocksureness, but 'assurance', as Evangelicals have learned to call it, when it is genuine has no such unattractiveness about it and actually goes along with a humble recognition of the mercy of God. It was commended by the Reformers in the sixteenth century, worked out in considerable detail and urged on Christians as their birthright by the Puritans of the seventeenth century, preached about and rejoiced in by the leaders of the Evangelical Revival in the eighteenth century, and held out as an integral element of Christian experience by Evangelicals in the last century and in this. Evangelicals have always made much of both the doctrine and the experience. In the first place, stress is laid on inner conviction of the truth of the Gospel as a recognizably consistent ingredient of faith and, in the second place, on an assurance of one's own salvation, the two aspects belonging together as the two sides of a single coin. Such conviction or assurance is the work of the Holy Spirit who opens hearts and minds to God's truth, and witnesses to believers that they are children of God (Romans 8.15,16). In the hands of the best exponents the doctrine has been set within its proper context of the struggle of the life of faith. We can take John Calvin as an example of this. For him, Christian assurance is the assurance of a person who in the midst of fears and cares is enabled to cast them on God and rise above them, while still feeling acutely the pressure of them. There is a struggle to be engaged in, but victory is certain. This is the constant experience of the Christian. So assurance is not easily come by though it is a part of true faith. In the seventeenth century, there were those who argued that full assurance of faith comes in only as the crown of a Christian's life experience. At all events, assurance is no quick and easy thing, any more than the faith to which it belongs is an easy option. Reference to the traditional Evangelical teaching on the whole subject is a good corrective to that rather superficial understanding which leads, for instance, new converts to think that they will be fully assured of the gospel and of their own salvation uninterruptedly from the time of their conversion onwards. Dr. Max Warren writing about the Evangelical Revival in the Church of England in the latter half of the eighteenth century and the first half of the nineteenth century, comments on the danger of allowing the understanding of assurance to degenerate into the introspective assessment of feeling:

'The paradox of Evangelicalism, as of all forms of spiritual religion, is that its strongest point is its weakest point. This point in Evangelical religion is to be found in the doctrine of assurance. The power of Evangelical religion is never more clearly seen than when the objective certainty of Christ's atoning, reconciling, victorious work, revealed in his own person as crucified and risen, lays its grasp on a man's soul, and then with compelling energy draws him out to bringing others to the Saviour. The insipidity of Evangelical religion is discovered in a doctrine of assurance which has degenerated into a cultivation of feelings, when the reliance is laid not upon an objective Gospel but upon a subjective experience'.

Such a degeneration is avoided when it is understood that assurance is precisely 'the assurance of faith' and that faith looks away from itself to its object. Assurance lives only in the bosom of faith and faith lives only as it directs itself towards God. Assurance can quite properly be thought of as a kind of reflex in the heart and mind of a person who places full confidence in the historical action of God in Christ as having a direct bearing on his own eternal salvation. But, as I have said, faith has battles to fight.

This attachment to the doctrine of assurance has had marked effects on Evangelical spirituality. It has produced such features as these: (i) Directness of approach to God, as child to father (exemplified in the style of informal prayer both individual and corporate); (ii) A concern for the maintenance of such a relationship, leading (as, for instance, in John Owen) to a marked stress on the mortification of known sin; (iii) Confidence in evangelism and in witness in general, turning inward assurance into active participation in the life of the world (as, for instance, in Evangelical social action). In these respects the doctrine has conferred great benefits. It does so still, but it must be well understood and carefully expressed. Here again, Evangelicals need to explore their *theological* heritage.

3

On Being Sustained

Beginning and Continuing

At intervals during past decades troublesome questions have arisen in the Church of England and in other churches too about the theory and practice of Christian initiation. For instance, is it right to baptize infants? If it is, what pastoral measures should be adopted to ensure as far as possible that the parents and godparents take their responsibilities with sufficient understanding and proper seriousness? The Baptists do not, of course, face this particular issue though, as they say themselves, their own practice has its problems. Evangelicals are not alone among Anglican people in feeling the pressure of these questions, but their own emphasis upon conversion and personal commitment has tended to give the questions for them an added sharpness and urgency. It would probably be true to say that for a very long period many Evangelicals in the Church of England, while going along with the church's stance on the baptism of infants and having their own children baptized, have sat rather loosely to the sacrament in its doctrinal significance, seeing it more as an opportunity for Christian parents publicly to 'dedicate' their child to God than as a sacrament of God's gracious initiative, claiming a person as his own. The increasingly 'secular' nature of modern society has sharpened the whole question for many, in that they find it hard to square their understanding of baptism with the actual practice of parishes where children of non-churchgoing people are baptized, their unease hardly being minimized by the good pre-baptismal preparation which is often given. This is not the place to enter into that debate. The point to notice here is that the *practice* of baptism in these days leaves many Church of England people confused and perplexed, and not Evangelicals only. They for their part lay great stress on conversion, as I have said, which they understand in terms of personal trust in and commitment to Christ, marked by repentance and the entrance upon a new life of worship and service. This is the event (be it long or short in duration) which signalizes the initiation of a person of whatever age into the family of God. When people are thus converted rarely is reference made to the relation of that experience to the sacrament of baptism unless the person was unbaptized when the conversion took place and baptism was clearly 'on the agenda' for the person's future admission to the Christian fellowship. Evangelical doctrine has certainly brought the two things into the closest possible relationship, but the understanding of the matter among Evangelicals in general has not always mirrored this good New Testament teaching. It can justifiably be said that baptism in the breadth and depth of its sacramental significance has not played the part it ought to have played in the Evangelical conception of what is involved in becoming a Christian. Professor C.F.D. Moule has put his finger on a relevant point here when he writes:

> 'We need not be surprised…if the many aspects of a single complex event, which concerns our entire personality in relation to other persons and to God, are sometimes (as we say) "staggered": they are successive and separated, rather than simultaneous and unified. But they all belong together…' (A Chosen Vessel, p.18).

Although conversion may be separated in time from our baptism which may well have taken place when we were infants, the two 'events' must be seen as belonging inextricably together in the pattern of God's grace towards us and our response to him. The point has been made again and again in the Evangelical tradition. Has it been taken on board adequately in the area of Evangelical spirituality? The matter is given proper perspective when another point which Evangelicalism has traditionally insisted on is kept in prominence, namely that baptism speaks not just at the 'one-off' moment of its administration but through the whole of a Christian's life. It says, in effect, that the baptized person is God's child and is therefore called to live day by day for God in union with the Christ who died and rose again for him/her and in the power of the Spirit. When this is grasped, conversion is seen as the outworking of the very meaning of baptism, and the conversion itself can more readily be appreciated (as it should be appreciated) as a decisive turning to God which nevertheless is reaffirmed again and again, and in a sense continued through life to the very end. Writing about the Christian's seeking for Christ, Martin Luther said this:

> 'But once found, he wants to be still further sought for and again and again to be found. We find him when we are converted to him from our sins and we seek him as we persevere in this conversion'.

There is a call to continue, to persevere, to 'turn' again and again. Baptism is a summons to that continuance. 'Beginning' and 'continuing' are really all of a piece in the mystery of baptism and its lifelong sequel.

Holy Communion in the Evangelical Tradition

Reform of patterns of worship in the contemporary Church of England has brought the sacrament of Holy Communion back into the centre of church life thus correcting a situation in which for many Evangelical congregations the sacrament had for a long time worn the appearance of an optional extra. The custom of the early Church which the Reformers in the sixteenth century made strenuous efforts to restore, was one Eucharist each Lord's day, at which all believers should be present, when the Word of God would be ministered to them through preaching and sacrament. Until the recent recovery of the centrality of the sacrament in Evangelicalism it was not unusual to find in parish churches Holy Communion celebrated at 8 o'clock on a Sunday morning (and that not every Sunday in all cases) with comparatively few communicants, while Morning and Evening Prayer were the main services of the day and much better attended. One would frequently find a shortened Prayer Book service of Holy Communion held after Morning or Evening Prayer on certain Sundays of the month, presenting the unedifying spectacle of the majority of the congregation at the first service leaving before the second. After Morning Prayer, some took coffee in the church hall while others took bread and wine in the sanctuary! Historically, Evangelicalism in the Church of England, certainly from the eighteenth century Revival but earlier as well, recognized the importance of eucharistic worship. In his book *Strange Victory*, the late Dr. Max Warren has a chapter on the Evangelical heritage in which he cites the attitude to the Holy Communion of a number of leading Evangelicals in the late eighteenth and early nineteenth centuries including Charles Simeon, Daniel Wilson, Edward Bickersteth and Basil Woodd. All had a 'high' view of the sacrament and urged those in their care to use it regularly and reverently. To mention just one example of the effect of their teaching, the result of Daniel Wilson's ministry, first in the Oxford village of Worton and then in the London parish of Islington, was a steady increase in the number of communicants. Warren records:

'Some time during 1827 or 1828 the number of communicants at Islington Parish Church had so grown that we read in the record of this period that "an early Sacrament at 8 o'clock" in addition to the usual celebration had been commenced'.

We should note here that the 8 o'clock celebration was *additional* to the customary provision. It would be true to say, therefore, that the modern reassertion in Evangelical circles of the centrality of the sacrament is but a recovery of one of the elements of the tradition.

Two documents of recent years representing Evangelical opinion in the Church of England give us a sense of what has been happening. The official Statement of the National Evangelical Anglican Congress held at Keele University in 1967 contains this:

'...we have let the sacrament be pushed to the outer fringes of church life, and the ministry of the Word be divorced from it. Small Communion services have been held seemingly at random, often more than one a Sunday, and the whole local church seldom or never comes together at the Lord's Table...We determine to work towards a practice of a weekly celebration of the sacrament as the central corporate service of the Church...' (Statement, p.35).

A decade later Trevor Lloyd sets out a 'model' in which he imagines what the local church congregation might look like in a few years' time but he's obviously drawing on the experience of current developments. In respect of eucharistic worship he writes:

> 'the large church meeting on Sunday morning is always Euchar-
> istic...it's a weekly celebration — and sometimes a pretty noisy one as
> people...use the different gifts God has given them for worship'
> (*Obeying Christ in a Changing World: 2 The People of God*, one of the
> books published in connection with the second National Evangelical
> Anglican Congress held at Nottingham in 1977).

It would seem that in the 90s the intention expressed in these two places
is being fulfilled quite widely (I'm not sure about the noise level!), though
there are considerable differences of style. The unifying factor is the Evangelical understanding of the sacrament as a 'visible word', the gospel of God set
forth, brought close and held out to the believing communicant who, in
receiving, truly participates in Christ himself and all the benefits of his pas-
sion. At the same time, in the same action of receiving the bread and wine, a
communicant expresses his or her dedication of life. We may reasonably
hope that in the future the Holy Communion will become even more sig-
nificant than it is already in the spiritual life of Evangelical church people.

'Biblical Personalism' in Prayer

In contrast with those sorts of religion which look on prayer as primarily
a matter of relating to God as 'ground of being', and stress the journey
inwards and the practice of contemplation, Evangelical religion regards
prayer as a reaching out to the personal God, as entering into dialogue with
him so that the emphasis tends to be upon petitionary prayer, though adoration and contemplation are not excluded. Sometimes the Evangelical stance
has been described as 'biblical personalism' by which is meant that relationship between God and ourselves which sees the human attributes of
thought and will and feeling as a reflection of the nature of God himself
though in him they are so fully realized that it is impossible for us to com-
prehend them (i.e. grasp them wholly with our minds). So when we pray to
God as our loving heavenly Father we are recognizing that he is truly personal and that therefore it is not far-fetched or inappropriate to think of ourselves as 'conversing' with him. In this context petition and intercession
have been the order of the day, following the teaching of Jesus who bade
people ask and go on asking for themselves and for others. In my own experience over many years prayer groups had this character. More recently,
there has been a larger place given to adoration. When meetings begin with
singing one quite often finds that this is described as a period of 'worship'
and the songs will be chosen so as to give expression to the participants'
awareness of the greatness, holiness, kindness, etc., of God (though there is
the danger in this way of describing the singing that 'worship' will come to
be thought of too narrowly — one is surely worshipping when one is lis-

tening to God in, for instance, Bible reading and exposition, and indeed in all life's activities). 'Biblical personalism' underlies all Evangelical teaching about prayer, which tries to be properly trinitarian, prayer being offered to the Father, through the mediation of the Son and Saviour, in the strength and enlightening of the ever present Holy Spirit. The personal relationship involved is of the order described in Exodus 33.11 where it is said that, 'the Lord would speak with Moses face to face, just as a man speaks with his friend'. Characteristic of Evangelical prayer has been the tenacity and perseverance which the phrase 'wrestling with God' describes. Another phrase — 'pouring out the heart to God' — describes the prayer which brings to God one's deepest and most urgent desires, a beseeching of him, a pleading with him, in which as a child to a loving father the suppliant presents his/ her petitions with confidence that he will listen and understand. But, somewhat paradoxically, because both the Bible and Christian experience require it, there is in this prayer a readiness to 'give way' to God, to recognize that his will is perfect. In all this, the Evangelical approach to prayer shows its difference from those ways of prayer which advocate stillness and the focusing of the mind on the divine nature. 'Divine-human encounter', to borrow the title of a book by Emil Brunner, would be a good way of characterizing the Evangelical understanding of what is happening when Christians pray.

Evangelicalism and Mysticism

Can it accurately be said that there is a 'mystical' element in Evangelical religion? It would appear that it can, if by 'mystical' is meant the experience of being in touch with God, or being aware of his presence. God has not confined such experience to people of any particular tradition of the Church. He 'comes' and relates himself in this immediate kind of way to people right across the spectrum of ecclesiastical and spiritual traditions. He 'comes' and enters into personal relationship with all who are open to receive him whether the experience has this kind of 'directness' or not. Indeed, the sense of the presence of God which most Christians have is only very occasionally heightened to the level of intensity that most people mean when they speak of 'mystical experience', but a real relationship is present nonetheless and a genuine knowledge of God is enjoyed. When we refer to 'mysticism' we ought to realize we are referring to a highly complex and many-sided phenomenon. The term is really an umbrella word. That aspect of mysticism which seems to characterize it across many of its manifestations and which has come in for a lot of criticism in Reformed and Evangelical circles is its reliance upon experience. This has been the basis for the virtual dismissal of it by some writers. Benjamin Warfield, the great American Reformed theologian who died in 1921, seized on precisely this point and at the end of a vigorous attack had this to say: 'We may be mystics or we may be Christians. We cannot be both. And the pretension of being both usually veils defection from Christianity'. In the article from which this comes, he is charging mysticism with conferring authority on experience (feeling, etc.), whereas he argues that authority resides only in revelation which means what God has said and done as recorded in Holy Scripture. True knowledge of God comes through Scripture and not through reflection on what is going on inside the human heart and mind. The article is a good treatment of the place of feeling within the Christian faith quite apart from its thrust against mysticism. However, it could be argued that its handling of mysticism is over-generalized and pays no attention to the fact that the great Christian mystics interpreted their experience, including their 'paranormal' experiences, in the light of the Church's faith to which they were completely committed. If St. John of the Cross has little to say about the Church and the sacraments this does not mean that he sat loose to them. If he does not concentrate his attention on the teaching of Scripture concerning our Lord's life and death and resurrection, this should not be taken to imply that it was unimportant to him. His chosen agenda (rather perhaps the agenda chosen for him by those who looked to him for spiritual guidance) caused him to write at length about the soul's progress to God which involved him in talking about spiritual states (with, it should be said, constant reference to Scripture according to the manner of his day). And it was he who wrote in the *Ascent of Mount Carmel*:

> '...he that would...seek any vision or revelation, would not only be acting foolishly, but would be committing an offence against God, by not setting his eyes altogether upon Christ'.

About Teresa of Avila, John's older contemporary, Rowan Williams says,

> 'she cannot easily be claimed as a proponent of the authority of experience...That men and women deceive themselves about their awareness of God is axiomatic for her...Individual experience, however vivid and compelling, has no authority as such: it is to be rigorously tested, with friends and confidantes, and with those officially charged with conserving the Church's teaching, the *letrados* ['lettered ones'] among the clergy'.

The truth is that 'mysticism' is a very diverse phenomenon in the Church about which it is dangerous to generalize. Each mystic ought to be evaluated in the light of the needs of his/her own time and with due reference to the total thrust of his/her belief and teaching.

But, this said, it is undoubtedly the case that Christian mysticism in general does stress the interior life and does encourage reflection on spiritual states, sometimes to the extent of finding an authority there which competes with the authority of the publicly given divine revelation. Evangelicalism for its part has always stressed the primacy of Holy Scripture while at the same time urging on Christians the need to interiorize the truth contained there. Some in the tradition have indeed tended to make too much of their experience but the tradition itself has been quite clear that experience is precisely the experience of faith, and faith lays hold of a reality which is over against it, distinct from it, and has authority over it. In this framework it has been possible for Christian experience to be urged as highly important and necessary without giving it a place in the determination of the knowledge of God which it ought not to occupy. So if we are going to talk about a 'mystical' element in Evangelical religion we should be careful to explain that what we have in mind is the 'experience of faith', that experience of the living God which comes through trusting in the One who revealed himself in Christ and redeemed the world in Christ and who makes real in the present by his Holy Spirit the great divine accomplishment which Scripture records.

4

On Being Renewed

Holiness Teaching

That the stress on holiness of life which had an important place in Evangelical teaching from the Reformation onwards has not been as obvious as it might have been in recent years is admitted on all sides. It could be argued that the success of the Evangelical wing of the Church in becoming genuinely and practically involved in social issues, and the concentration on evangelistic activity from the 1950s onwards, along with (in the Church of England at least) a preoccupation with forms of worship and with questions of order, have deflected attention from what historically has been a central thrust of the tradition. The Reformers laid the foundation for subsequent Evangelical handling of the matter. John Calvin rings the changes on the vocabulary he uses. He is often speaking about one or another aspect of sanctification when he refers to repentance, new life, conversion, and mortification. His conception of the matter is, in brief, that sanctification consists in the first place in the consecration of the individual to God, which in turn inevitably leads to a progressive renunciation of all those things which disrupt a believer's relationship with God and also to a day-to-day cleansing of the believer from the pollution of sin. He thinks of it as a gradual process which will be completed only in heaven at the end of a journey which involves a hard disciplining of the self. The Puritans in the following century developed this further. The great John Owen spelled out the necessity (on the positive side) of attitudes and actions which express faith and love towards God and (on the negative side) of a determined assault on all those states of mind and heart, and all those inclinations and habits, which lead away from God and the fulfilling of his will. 'The whole work', he says, 'is by degrees to be carried on towards perfection all our days', but the work will only be accomplished by the Holy Spirit working in us. With John Wesley the doctrine underwent a further development. He taught a 'Scriptural holiness' (his term for it) which held out the hope and possibility of 'perfect love'. The teaching aroused a good deal of controversy then and has done so since. One hears little of it in modern Methodism, but in the eighteenth century and later (in some circles) the teaching was undoubtedly influential. Reaction from it which set in during the latter part of the eighteenth century and the first part of the nineteenth century led to what appeared to some to be a very gloomy view of the Christian life, in which it seemed that all that could be expected was a constant failure to overcome sin and a consequent lack of confidence in the Spirit's power. So it was (to recount the history in a disgracefully cursory fashion) that new 'holiness movements' emerged ('Higher Life', 'Victorious Life', etc.) among them, in England, the Keswick movement, a movement which is still alive and flourishing and which has exercised a great influence on Protestant Christianity across the world. Keswick teaching has been sharply criticized and it is the case that over the years aspects of it, such as the 'second blessing' (seen as the reception of grace to overcome sin) and the call for passivity in the hands of a gracious God so that he may do his sanctifying work in a fully receptive soul, have given rise to concern. As to 'entire sanctification' Keswick seems never to have taught it and has thus avoided the convolutions of doctrine made by those who tried to hold it yet at the same time had to face up to the brute facts of experience. In recent years it would appear that the general drift of the teaching avoids the pitfalls which some have critically noted. At the Convention in 1986 the Chairman of the Council, the Rev. Philip Hacking, speaking on Galatians 5, referred to some of the major criticisms in these words:

'It is said in some books that there was a day when a doctrine was preached at Keswick which suggested that you "let go and let God", and you entered into a realm where from now on it would always be peace. You'd moved from Romans 7 with its battle, into Romans 8 with its victory; and you'd never go back to Romans 7. I don't know whether that was preached here; it hasn't been in my time. But if it was, I think — with great respect to our forefathers — it was unbiblical. Though there is no suggestion in the New Testament that I can enter in by a kind of passive resignation, and from now on, in the life in the Spirit, the conflict is gone. But it does not say what lots of Christians seem to experience, that it's just one grim battle. Oh no! There is a battle, but there is victory!'

The question that faces Evangelicalism today is : How can this historic concern for holiness (itself thoroughly biblical) be revived? Evangelicals have (rightly to my mind) largely thrown over the petty restrictions which may at one time have had a real point as protests against prevailing social evils. There is today a healthier attitude towards participation in and enjoyment of the good things which God has created or enabled human beings to create. But, as always, there is the accompanying danger that Christians will fail to take seriously the need for honest recognition of the insidious effect of worldly standards and expectations upon their own lives. There is also the danger that unreflective actions will blunt the Christian's conscience in respect of personal sin and the need to repent of it and be forgiven for it.

The subject 'holiness' is a complicated one, but if Evangelicalism is to be true to its inheritance it must once again take the whole matter with the utmost seriousness in both its theological and its practical aspects. Faithfulness to the Bible requires nothing less.

The Renewal Movement

Along with many other branches and groupings in the Christian Church Evangelicalism has been deeply influenced in recent decades by what has come to be known as 'the Charismatic Movement'. While Evangelicalism in both its Puritan and Wesleyan expressions spoke much of the work of the Holy Spirit in conversion and sanctification, lately a prominence has been given to the Spirit's working in the Church and in the individual which has revived these classical emphases and caused Evangelicals to be more aware of and more open to the Spirit in their own Christian living. Much good has flowed from this, but it has not been without its difficulties. At the level of theology (or should one say 'pneumatology"?) Evangelicals have been somewhat divided over issues like the baptism of the Spirit, the place of glossolalia, the validity of modern day prophecy, etc. But in the judgment of this one observer of the scene, it has been a great blessing in that issues right across the doctrinal spectrum have been looked at afresh and new insights have been obtained to the benefit of Evangelicals of various sorts. The recovery (for that is what it seems to have been) of interest in the doctrine of the Holy Spirit, his person and his work, has directed people's attention to many truths of which the passage of time had perhaps dulled their perception. One might include here the doctrines of conviction of sin, conversion, witness of the Spirit and adoption into the family of God, the priesthood of all believers expressed in terms of the use of spiritual gifts, and the call, implicit in all true Christian discipleship, to holiness of life. In the area of spirituality, there has been experienced refreshment in private prayer, a new desire to listen to God's Word in the Bible and a new delight in doing so, a renewed awareness of the immanence of God in his world and people's lives, a greater confidence in Christian witness. As far as the church scene is concerned, Evangelicals along with many others have gained a new sense of enjoyment in worship, and an appreciation of the need for greater freedom and flexibility in liturgical forms. Undoubtedly a lot of this has gone hand in hand with social and cultural change in society at large but that is not a new phenomenon in the history of the Church (!) and it is actually necessary if the Church is to relate to people where they are and look and sound like a contemporary movement. As long as the Church holds fast to its title deeds and develops its life in consonance with its received tradition nothing but good can come.

One of the most interesting outcomes of the widespread Renewal Movement is that a number of practices, long familiar to Evangelicals, have been adopted by people of other traditions. An obvious example is the 'prayer meeting', an occasion for reading the Bible, for sharing concerns, and for praying extemporarily. In the opposite direction, Evangelicals participating in the Renewal in company with Christians of other traditions have learned much about those traditions and discovered the joy of engaging in praise and prayer across the old denominational boundaries.

A 'Worldly' Spirituality

There is a sense in which every brand of spirituality, the Evangelical included, is 'other worldly', in that it is directed to realities which are largely unseen. It is also true to say that Evangelical spirituality has been developed in the context of the world's life; it is an 'everyday' spirituality, a spirituality of the home, the factory, the shop, and the school. This has been one of its most obvious marks from the Reformation onwards. Against the view which had been previously widespread though not universal, that 'true' spirituality can be worked out only in a monastic or semi-monastic setting, Evangelical spirituality set about hammering out a way of devotion and obedience which was not only suited to life in the world but derived much of its inspiration from that life. That is to say, life in the world was seen as belonging to the very stuff of prayer, informing it and fuelling it, so that God's providential presence and control of all things was kept constantly in view and rejoiced in. It is in this sense that we can call this spirituality 'worldly'.

How has it functioned? Two features of it are very important. First, there has been a disciplined attempt to carve out of each day's activities space for prayer and Bible reading (frequently along with other spiritual reading). In recent years some Evangelicals have taken a leaf out of the book of their Catholic friends and gone on retreat from time to time. The setting aside of time for prayer and reading has been recognized as necessary though the difficulty of doing so has been shown up by the frequency of exhortations in print and from the pulpit to keep up the practice. Secondly, there has been a conscious attempt to translate the insights gained in prayer and reading into action. 'Obedience' has been a regular watchword. Evangelical social action, as exemplified in the lives of notable people like Shaftesbury and Wilberforce, sprang from just this understanding of the 'obedience of faith'. Prayer in private or in the family circle or in a group of friends would take up the issues of daily life. There was an emphasis on God's activity in the world and in the lives of individuals. While personal holiness, promoted by a close walk with God, was sought after, the abiding emphasis was on God's direction of one's life and his fatherly management of one's personal, social, and business activities. Holiness was indeed seen as a relationship to God which was best enhanced by meeting him in the everyday world rather than by withdrawal from it to find him in some separated sphere.

As for Bible reading, this was understood as the prime means of deriving guidance from God for ordinary life. Here were found inspiration and encouragement through observing the lives of Bible characters and through listening to those parts of the Bible which offer direction for Christian living. If the text was not always properly understood in regard to its historical setting, it was at least always treated with the greatest reverence and was expected to yield its treasures to all who were in earnest.

Ways and Means

Evangelicals are looking outside their own tradition for guidance in the spiritual life. Such is the assertion that is occasionally made by those who have a wide knowledge of the Evangelical constituency. Undoubtedly some are, and are finding that there are things on offer which go with their own tradition and, if anything, add depth to it. That seems to be the case, for instance, with the use being made of 'Ignatian Spirituality' where in retreats and in private prayer Evangelicals are deriving benefit from the commended methods of Bible meditation. I believe it would be unfortunate if such cross-tradition experience were frowned upon or discouraged. But the trend (if trend it is) should cause Evangelicals to ask questions about the way they are drawing or not drawing on their own spiritual tradition. Their *practice* has some hardy features which have stood the test of time, such as prayer meetings and fellowship groups, and their emphasis upon the nexus between preaching the Bible from the pulpit and reading it at home has undergirded all their devotional life. But they seem to be deficient, at any rate in these days, in offering individuals clear guidance on the spiritual life, which is probably why some have gone elsewhere for such advice. Exhortations to prayer and Bible study have not been lacking and hints on the use of the 'Quiet Time' have appeared in print occasionally, but practical, individually tailored, help has been rather conspicuously absent. It has been too readily assumed that Evangelical people *know* how to say their prayers and will keep going without recourse to help from others. Now no-one, I hope, would want to advocate a stereotyped syllabus of methods to which all should adapt themselves. That would be self-defeating. Rather what is needed is some way whereby individuals within the tradition can be helped with their particular problems. No-one wants to create problems where there are none but it would seem that more attention ought to be given to the questions which people ask, theological and other, like: How can I get the best out of my daily Bible reading? What am I to make, in terms of God's dealings with me, of those times of darkness when prayer seems to be a waste of time? What is the theological rationale of intercession? How can I keep fresh my prayers for people I've never seen and for causes that are large and complex? We need more literature on the spiritual life from an Evangelical perspective, and it would be good to have some of the literary riches of the tradition from past centuries served up in readable form (perhaps summarized) so as to make them more attractive and usable by today's Christians. We also need something akin to what in other traditions is called 'Spiritual Direction' or 'Counselling'. When (as is usually the case these days) this means the giving of general guidance and advice, it is nothing to be afraid of. It has of course happened in an informal way among Evangelicals for centuries when, for instance, pastors have offered spiritual help to those who have asked for it. But is there enough of it today? Again, might there not be more use made of study days/evenings/week-ends when the treasures of Evangelical spirituality could be explored in some depth? Evangelicalism has been good at promoting groups for Bible study and prayer; these have been one of its notable strengths. Might not questions of spirituality be tackled in businesslike fashion by extending arrangements such as these? And could not more opportunities be provided for retreats and quiet days conducted by Evangelicals for Evangelicals — and for all who would like to participate? The suggestion ought not to be regarded as partisan but simply as a way of providing a stimulus *within Evangelicalism* towards what is already widely used by other traditions in the Church with manifest profit. And last but by no means least, ought not spirituality to figure more prominently in Evangelical theological education?

What now should be said about the wide range of techniques and practices on offer these days which so many use and regard as the very stuff of spirituality? Chris Hingley in an article entitled, 'Evangelicals and Spirituality' published in *Themelios* in April/May 1990, helpfully shows that techniques may well be entirely neutral in tendency and therefore usable by Christians who want to be helped to satisfy their 'genuine hunger for God'. But he issues warnings, especially about the danger of regarding techniques as, in themselves, a way of intimacy with God, so that revealed truth is bypassed and use of the mind depreciated. He writes,

> '...if such techniques have any value at all, it must be recognised that it is only a limited one. It is dangerous to confuse them with prayer: at best, they can be only a preparation for prayer'.

He has in mind techniques such as those which promote concentration, like fixing attention on breathing and listening to all the sounds in the immediate environment, and so on. In an increasingly stressful age the proliferation of books and groups inculcating practices of relaxation and recollection is perfectly understandable. Many of these practices are religiously neutral and are obviously helpful to those who use them, and there is no reason why they should not be useful to Christians as long as they know what they are doing and what the differences are between these things and the spiritual relationship with God to which they as Christians are committed. Hingley quotes Simon Tugwell:

> 'The earliest known use of the Latin word spiritualitas remains very close to what St. Paul meant by "spiritual"...Christians, by virtue of their baptism, are meant to be "spiritual" in the sense that they are meant to be "led by the Spirit" and to "live by the Spirit"'.

This is well said. We might add that it implies being a constantly attentive listener to the Word, the incarnate Word himself and the Word of Holy Scripture which testifies to him. If a technique helps the Christian to live in this responsive way it is wholesome. Danger arises when people try to hear God speaking to them apart from the revelation he has given, or make no attempt to test against that revelation what they ostensibly hear him saying to them.

5

What of the Future?

The Evangelical spiritual tradition like every other spiritual tradition that has real life in it is a growing and developing thing. Like the Christian faith itself of which it is one expression, it moves on through time interacting with its environment in Church and world, drawing upon its historical resources and adapting itself so as to continue viable and lively in the new conditions that arise. This does not or should not mean that it loses its character and parts company with its roots. Recent books like Alister McGrath *Roots that*

Refresh, and J.I. Packer *Among God's Giants*, are powerful dissuasives to that. There is, of course a danger in this tradition as in all other traditions that people become so busy managing change that they forget what it is that has to be preserved in the midst of the changing. But the other danger can be just as deadly: the danger of a conservatism which steadfastly refuses to move forward, to think again, to experiment, to modify. Such conservatism needs to be confronted with the great Reformation principle of *ecclesia reformanda est*, in the light of Scripture, as Scripture is earnestly studied and applied to every aspect of the Church's life including its spiritual life. Was it not the Puritan, John Robinson, who declared: 'The Lord hath more truth yet to break forth out of his holy word'? It is surely precisely as Christians are confronted with new challenges and opportunities and made to *think* that fresh insights from Scripture and tradition come to them. I am saying that the Evangelical spiritual tradition must not stand still, busy only in digging into its past and becoming engrossed with past glories. That is the way to fossilization and irrelevance.

What does this mean in practice? I would urge two things. First a sufficient acquaintance by Evangelicals with the tradition and a grateful enjoyment of what it has to offer (which will involve reading books like those mentioned and, where possible, the actual writings of the great exponents of Evangelical spirituality, or summaries of them). Secondly, a readiness to look seriously at other traditions and to learn from them. In doing this it will certainly emerge that in some instances caricatures rather than actualities have determined Evangelical attitudes (e.g. that a Christian mystic like St. John of the Cross undermines the primacy of divine grace in his description of the 'ascent' to God). And, as I have said elsewhere in this booklet, benefit may be derived from various techniques and spiritual approaches on offer today provided that the great *theological* emphases of the Evangelical tradition are not obscured. I have already suggested some practical ways of promoting the spiritual life of Evangelical Christians. There are certainly many others. It will be good to remember (what was said in the Introduction) that Evangelicalism derives its character, its 'ethos', not so much from particular things which make it distinctive or mark it off from other traditions, but from its bringing together into a coherent structure of doctrine and practice, a number of emphases, many of which are found elsewhere; which should prompt an 'openness' to other traditions, a rejoicing in the recognition of a lot of common ground, and a willingness to receive light from wherever it comes. Evangelicals will go on believing that the Bible is the chief source of nourishment for the spiritual life and they will want to test every new insight against its teaching. But they will do this as those who realize that God's truth and God's ways are such that they can never be fully explored by *any* one tradition no matter how vigorous and venerable.